Lost in Love

The GPS to a Christian Relationship

By Sean Sarvis

Dedication & Acknowledgements

I would like to dedicate this book first and foremost to my Lord and Savior Jesus Christ who blessed me with insight and understanding.

He blessed me with the vision and the ability to write this book. It was through the ups and downs of life and relationships that I gained wisdom.

I also dedicate this book to my mother Linda Walker, who raised me to be the man that I am today.

She had to do it by herself. She didn't have a guide, a map or GPS and I am blessed to have a strong woman like her in my life.

I would also like to thank my pastors, Rev. Dr. Grainger Browning, Jr and his lovely wife, Rev. Dr. Jo Ann Browning, of Ebenezer AME church. They have been my pastors for 30 years and I am blessed to know them.

God has blessed me through them.

They allow God to speak through them. Many of the scriptures that I live by and the things that I remember I was taught under their ministry.

I'm blessed to have them in my life.

I would like to thank Rev. Tony Lee and the Lee family of Community of Hope, AME Church. It was through their Young Adult ministry that I was able to grow as a Christian man.

I was able to see and recognize things that I mention in the book. I would like to thank the current pastor of the church as well, Rev. Vernon Ware.

Most importantly, I would like to dedicate this book to my three daughters. Anything is possible if you trust God and believe in yourself.

Foreword

By Mrs. Stacy Lattisaw – Jackson

Knowing Sean Sarvis has been quite the blessing! I have always admired not only his unique humor, but more important, his walk with the Lord.

He and I have had many conversations over the years as it relates to his decision to use his gift of comedy in a manner unprofane, and in such a way as to be inclusive of all people from any walk of life.

Sean's hilarious humor, kindness and heart to entertain his audiences with Christian humor is truly remarkable.

Lost in Love: Sean's GPS to a Christian Relationship, delves into many facets of his personal dating experiences.
As important, Sean sheds light on how to handle dating "snafus" and gives insight into recognizing pitfalls before they occur using Christian principles and the word of God for guidance.

This book is both informative and notably humorous.

It is a quick read and one I recommend to anyone seeking guidance in their own relational experiences, and to those who wish to infuse Christian values into their dating experiences.

Table of Contents

Dedication & Acknowledgements 2

Foreword 4

Love 11

My Story 15

The New Sexy.. 17

Get with Your Own Kind 21

Dangerous Dating 25

The Red Flags 31

The Dating Dilemma 36

Communication 42

Dating Their Kids 52

The Great Debate 57

Purpose in a Relationship 64

The Unique Relationship...................................... 70

Sex & Lust 75

Temptation 84

Spirits and Sex.. 90

Masturbation.. 92

Jealousy 98

Social Media 101

Baggage & Forgiveness 110

It's My Time... 115

About the Author 119

Thank you for purchasing my book. I wrote this book because I have always been a fan and an admirer of love.

God made us out of love and he made us to love one another.

I was raised in a single parent household. I have absolutely no recollection of my parents being together.

I never saw love first hand. I would visit my friends and see their parents together.

As I got older, seeing couples that have been married for 10, 15, 20 years was amazing to me because I didn't see it first hand growing up.

Being married and divorced and based on the relationships that I have been through, I decided to give you my input on how Christian relationships should be.

This book is based on my mistakes and those that I have witnessed. I've witnessed all levels of relationships from dating to divorce.

I wanted to create a guide for those who grew up like I did and had questions about relationships.

I've always admired couples who could endure hardships, trials and tribulations and remain in love.

This book is for the single Christian and the married Christian.

I am not going to preach to you but I will provide scriptures to support my thoughts and beliefs on communication and love.

"Two are better than one, because they have a good return for their labor: if either of them falls down, one can help the other up. But pity anyone who falls and has no one to help them up."

Ecclesiastes 4:9-10 (NIV)

Love

Love…such a small powerful word. I don't care who you are; everyone loves to be in love.

Of course, there are such things as a Mother's love, Father's love, sibling love, grandparent's love, friendship love, and a love for music, a love of cars, a love of sports, and a love food.

I think you get my drift.

But there's nothing like being in love with that special person. That boyfriend or girlfriend, or just simply defined in the new-millennium, "my friend."

Love, in this case, will make you so high…higher than any drug available on the street, today.

I'm talking about the kind of love that makes you behave differently. Got you smiling and saying, "Hello" to everyone you see, *even those who you don't like.*

The love that makes you spend money you don't have.

You feel no pain when you're in this kind of love. You could be suffering from a toothache but as long as you got *your boo* around, you couldn't care less.

In so many words, this type of love is irreplaceable...there's truly nothing like it. Love is so great and special, that it shouldn't cost you anything.

Only thing it may cost is your heart, being broken, which is an unbearable pain that you can't remedy with medication.

Unlike a broken leg that can heal in about eight to ten weeks, a broken heart takes much longer. Heartbreak can literally change who you are, redefine you.

Millions of dollars have been made in the name of love, but much more has been made for the heartbroken.

Think about how many songs you hear on the radio where some heartbroken soul is crying their heart out in the name of love.

Poor love gets a bad rap if you ask me. "How can I be angry with love?" you ask. It's easy. You fall for someone's representative, and I do mean hard. Then you get married and things change.

I'm not saying marriage changes things, but it added more pressure onto an already tense situation, but I'll get into that later.

The purpose of this book is to help you understand love and relationships better. I want you to know how I, Sean Sarvis survived heartbreak and how you can too.

You're in for a real treat here, I'm going to tell you my testimony and give you some tips on how not to make the same mistakes I made.

THE DEFINITION OF A PURE LOVE

Don't just pretend to love others. Really love them. Hate what is wrong. Hold tightly to what is good. Love each other with genuine affection, and take delight in honoring each other.

Romans 12:9-10

My Story

Alright, before I begin my story I want you to understand that I'm telling you this to help you. As church folk, we know how important it is to give and hear someone's testimony.

Your story shows others how God has delivered you from circumstances and encourages others that they too can be delivered from their situations.

My goal is to encourage you and show you how to have a successful, God-driven, relationship. I also would like this book to invoke discussion. I want you to read through this book and debate my thoughts with your partner or your friend. How will we grow together if we don't open the lines of communication?

Some of the topics in this book will open the door for more conversation, which is great. The more we talk the stronger our relationships will grow. You may also see some areas where I have posed questions for you. Please feel free to share your ideas or write your answers in the book.

This is a workbook. The goal is not to just read this book but to also take action. We all know that faith without works is dead.

Let's get moving.

Pull out your highlighter and your pen, because you are about to enter an exciting journey that you will want to remember.

The New Sexy

When I was in my twenties the word sexy meant a big butt, big breasts, nice eyes, a nice pair of legs and of course a cute face.

Well, over the years, as I matured my attention to certain things have changed. I no longer look for the physical attributes in a woman.

Okay let me correct that, I'm not saying that I have no standards, don't get me wrong. I'm just saying that now I look for compatibility and personal attributes as well as physical.

As humans, we always judge a person on the surface. As you have been told many times, men are visual creatures. We look at a woman's face and body first and decide where to take it from there.

But after dating a few too many beautiful disasters I know exactly what I need and it's not the pretty girl without goals, or the stunning statuesque girl who couldn't carry a conversation in a bucket. Despite popular opinion, you get used to a pretty face quickly. Big butts get too big, big breasts sag

and beauty fades. But the heart remains the same.
The heart doesn't change.

So, the new sexy for me is a clean house. Now,
I'm no neat freak but at least have some standards.
*I don't want to go to your house and you have
more dishes in your sink than in your cabinet.*

I'm also attracted to a prayer warrior. Fellas are
looking for a woman who is strong in her faith.
When the going gets tough I need a woman who
knows how to turn to God. She doesn't fall to the
ground in a crumbled heap.

She goes down on her knees and looks up to our
Lord and Savior for help. There's nothing like a
praying woman.

A woman who takes time out for her children, a
nurturing woman, a good mother is a part of the
new sexy.

I love to be with a woman who includes her
children, who thinks about them.

I have been out with women who turn their
children away when we're spending time together.
A Godly man is looking for an honest woman and
a supportive woman. We are attracted to women
who are ambitious and intelligent.

The man is the head of the household, but the woman is his rib.

A man needs to feel secure in the fact that you have the family as your second priority in life, behind God.

As the man of the house, we are obligated to do the same.

This is how our home stays protected and our relationship remains centered in God.

Be ye not unequally yoked together with unbelievers: for what fellowship hath righteousness with unrighteousness? And what communion hath light with darkness?

2 Corinthians 6:14

Get with Your Own Kind

If you are a Christian, it makes sense to want to date or court another Christian. This is much easier said than done. As people we are always attracted to someone who is different than ourselves.

Think about it. Many of the people you dated were completely different than you or had different upbringings.

That's what makes us unique, our story. The background of our lives define who we are.

None of our stories are exactly the same. This also makes it challenging with regards to relationships.

We are also attracted to those who we can't have. Boy, those situations can end very badly, yet those are the ones with the steamiest storyline.

Okay ladies, excuse me for a moment, I want to talk to the men.

How many times have you been trying to stand for God, then out of nowhere here she comes. A beautiful radiant woman, with a nice shape; smelling really good and speaking the language.

What language you ask?
Whatever language that gets your attention.

It doesn't have to be provocative, it could be subtle, but please believe the devil knows exactly what you like.

Remember the old saying, the devil doesn't come to you in horns and a tail he comes to you as everything you have ever wanted.

So men, if you are saved, and you ask this gorgeous creature, "Are you saved?"

When she responds, "no, who is this Jesus you speak of?" What do you do?

Now we know clearly where they stand with Jesus, but instead we start to make excuses for them. "Oh, I can teach her about God", "She will be fine." We will still have enthusiasm about the idea of being with this woman.

At some point in our lives we have all done this. The reason why we do this is because the person seems so exciting to us.

They're refreshing to us.

The other thing is we have that reassurance. The thought in the back of our mind, telling us, "I'm going to change him and save him."

In the book of Judges, there was a man named Sampson. Sampson had favor with God.

Sampson was whipping everything that came his way. Nothing could stop Sampson. Sampson took out thousands of men.

What led to Sampson's destruction?

A woman named Delilah. Sampson was an Israelite that had favor with God. Delilah was a Philistine.

Sampson could've had any Israelite woman he wanted, but he had to have Delilah.
We are the same way now. We have been saved all of our lives. We used to sing in the junior choir, we served on the usher board and was also a deacon or deaconess.

We served on the usher board for so long, our knees are now bad as a result of it.

We've served the Lord and the church our entire lives, but are attracted to the unsaved. We are attracted to the thugs, the hoochie mamas and just like Sampson it leads to destruction.

Well, someone might say, "I'm already saved…I am a believer…I can get them saved and everything will be great."

Think again.

If you desire to walk someone towards Christ, that's great. If you are trying to walk them for your own personal reasons, that's going to be an uphill battle for you.

Do nothing out of selfish ambition or vain conceit, but in humility consider others better than yourselves –Philippians 2:3

Ladies, it's your turn. You're out with your girls, having a good time and here he comes, tall dark and handsome. He will smell like your favorite cologne, saying the right things.

Like I said, the devil knows what you want.

Dangerous Dating

In order to find love we must first date. I don't know about you, but dating isn't really what it used to be.

When we're in our twenties dating is all about having fun and meeting a variety of different people.

Now that we are older, no one dates for fun anymore. Everyone is dating for marriage. I am no longer looking for a young lady to hang out with; I'm looking for someone I can build with.

The idea sounds great. Take a lady out; get to know her and the rest is history. These days, however, you have to be careful.

There are a lot of hurt people out there. There are also a lot of crazy people out there. You have to watch out for them. They start off as sweet as pie, then suddenly... you're filling out a restraining order.

Check this out....

I met a young lady through a mutual friend. She lived in Baltimore and at the time I lived in Capitol Heights. We talked on the phone a couple of times and finally decided to meet.

She drove to meet me and I decided to take her on a tour of Washington, DC. Since it was such a nice day outside, I took her to visit the monument and we enjoyed a nice lunch on the mall.

We had great conversation and I really felt like our date was a success. We danced to music on our way home and talked incessantly.

This girl was motivated and spoke of dreams of becoming an entrepreneur. She recently received her license in Cosmetology and planned to open her own shop.

I was a little disappointed when she announced that she was ready to head home. She didn't want to be on the road too late. We hugged and shared a nice intimate kiss.

When she left I turned Kem on the radio and imagined our next date. My ringing cell phone interrupted my thoughts. I didn't mind though because I knew it was her.

I answered the phone all sweet; "Hey" I said smiling to myself.

"Hey, B***h!" she yelled on the phone. I chuckled a little uneasy, wondering if she was kidding. "Girl, you're crazy" I said laughing to myself. "You thief!" she screamed into the phone.

At this point I don't know what to say. "What are you talking about?" I asked. She went into a tirade. "You're broke tail! You didn't have to steal money from me," she yelled.

Now, I have not been an angel my entire life, but one thing I have never been is a thief. I couldn't believe that this was happening.

This wasn't the girl I was with the entire day. She seemed so nice. I never imagined her angry let alone cursing me out on the phone.

"I don't have enough gas!" she screamed, "You took my gas money," she yelled accusingly. I didn't know what to do.

At first I laughed nervously, while looking around for Ashton Kutcher. I knew that I had to be on "Punk'd." This couldn't be real life. After a 20 second tirade, I finally interrupted her, "Come back over here and I'll take you to the gas station" I said as she hung up the phone in my ear.

I nervously chuckled to myself. "This can't be happening," I said as I tried to reassure myself. I heard a loud horn outside and looked out the window.

As I peeked through the blinds, I grabbed my cellphone and sent my mother a text. I told her the gas station that we were heading to, the girls name and her license plates number.

I know it sounds over the top but I absolutely had to let someone know where I was heading. I've watched too many Snapped episodes to not tell someone.

After my mother sent me a "got it" response, I smiled to myself. I took a deep breath and realized that I was working myself up for nothing.

Then I heard her car pull into the driveway and the loud, blaring horn.

Resisting the urge to turn the lights out and hide, I exited the house and walked towards her car. I climbed in the car and she burned rubber as she peeled out of the driveway.

That night everything on the side of the road looked interesting.

I was in the car wanting to blow steam on the windows and write, "Help Me." As we rode in silence, I began to wonder what I was doing in the car with the woman.

She had music blasting from the stereo and she was staring straight ahead, not even trying to look at me.

I paid for the gas and she took me back home, still in silence.

When she drove me back home, I opened the door and said, "I didn't steal from you" she looked at me and said, "Whatever, broke negro!" and pulled out of the driveway with the door still open.

I never heard from her again. I wondered if she ever found the twenty dollars that she swore I stole.

Today, I can laugh at that situation. I still wonder why I rode with her to the gas station.

I didn't date for a few weeks after that episode.

And this I pray, that your love may abound yet more and more in knowledge and in all judgment: that ye may approve things that are excellent: that ye may be sincere and without offence till the day of Christ.

Philippians 1: 9-10

The Red Flags

Okay, you've heard about my crazy date. I know you have some stories of your own that you're probably reminiscing about right now.

Hopefully, it's been long enough for you to laugh about it now.

When I speak of red flags, I'm talking about that God-given gut instinct that tells you that something just isn't right.

Hopefully your spirit of discernment is better than mine, but here are some red flags for you to look out for.

Have you ever been to someone's house and wanted to help them clean? I dated a woman who was so well put together; I just knew that I hit the jackpot.

My only complaint was about her cluttered car.

You know the people who have to move things off the seats before you can sit down. She was the type of person that had to move stuff off the seat and from the floor of the passenger side. There was my red flag, but did I heed the warning?

Nope!

She was an exceptional cook as well. She would bring dishes to my house that had me ready to propose.

I still haven't met a woman who could fry a pork chop like her. She seemed shy about where she lived.

I grew up in the hood, so I don't go around judging anyone's life or dwelling places, but I didn't press her about it.

Well early one morning she called my house, hysterical. "I just saw a mouse. I can't move," she whispered in fear.

Me being the man I am, I jumped at the chance to save this lovely damsel in distress.

I told her I was on my way as she gave me directions to her home. When I knocked at the door I heard a loud commotion and then the door swung open.
I stood at the doorway in utter shock. Her home was packed with furniture, newspapers and clutter.

It looked like an episode right out of, "Hoarders." I couldn't believe what I was seeing. I told her to go to the car as I tried to catch the creature.

She ran past me yelling, "I saw him in the kitchen" she said as she fled in fear.

I walked inside the kitchen and nearly vomited. The sink was filled with dirty dishes. Her floor was dirty and I could see an inch worth of grease on her stove.

I shuddered thinking about the meals that I devoured from her. The meals prepared in that dirty kitchen.

I tried my hardest to catch the mouse and prevent my gag reflex from taking over.

I heard a commotion in the cabinet under the sink and swung the door open; when I saw the roaches crawling I took off running out of the apartment. To this day, I don't remember what I said to her when I left the apartment. All I remember is driving on 95 South at 100 mph.

Have you ever met someone so crazy their family secretly warns you? Well, I was seeing this beautiful woman.

We dated for months and were really feeling each other.

She invited me to her grandparents' home for Thanksgiving dinner. We had a blast together, so I was really looking forward to meeting her family.

Well, I could sense something strange from the moment we walked inside the house. Everyone stared at me like I was an alien. She introduced me as her, "Fiancée."

Although, I was shocked by her admission, I didn't mind. I was really feeling this girl and her introduction told me that she was feeling me too.

I didn't pay attention to the fact that the family members were all giving me the side-eye. When we sat at the table and her father blessed the food, he said a special prayer for my girlfriend.

My interests peaked at that point.

Family members were offering their advice, left and right. "Make sure you slow down on those drinks," they warned as she sipped her first glass of wine.

I didn't know what to say, so I continued to eat and observe.

At least the food was good. Everyone asked her questions like, "So where are you living now?" and "Have you been taking your medicine?"

The evening grew from interesting to alarming, when her father pulled me aside and asked if she was continuing her 12-step program.

Often times you can learn a lot about someone based on how their family treats them.
If they grab their purses and start hiding their electronics, take heed to the warning signs.

Pay attention to how your date treats the waitress or waiter at the restaurant.

In my opinion, to really know someone you have to see them in a few tense situations.

Watch their temperament when a waitress makes a mistake on their order.

Take notice of how they behave when someone cuts them off, while driving.

If you really want to know how someone really is, have them use the Internet for fifteen minutes on a dial-up connection.

You will actually see someone for who they really are. It may sound silly, but you'll be thanking me later.

The Dating Dilemma

Everyone in life experiences times when they need to make decisions that they would rather avoid. Sometimes we enjoy the comfort zone.

We enjoy that which brings us stability.
In our quest for love we go through many ups and downs trying to find just the right one.
Being a man or woman of God makes this process ten times more difficult.

You want someone who is going to match you in faith; someone who can pray and minister to you when things get rough.

Although there are single people in the church there is often a level of un-comfortableness that turns you off.

You don't want to have a bad dating experience with someone that you also attend church.

Every time you look up she will be giving you serious side eye from the choir box. You can't even pray in peace. No, thank you.

Some would say that being a comedian makes things easier. I have met many different types of women while performing around the country.

It has been fun and strange at times.

I met one young lady at a show in North Carolina. We hung out a couple of times and since I had such a good time with her, I decided to take her with me to a show in Pennsylvania.

I love to laugh and she was a hilarious woman. She was funny without trying to be funny. She was beautiful too.

Dark skinned thick and natural hair. I love a woman who can accentuate her natural beauty. It's amazing what a woman can do with what God gave her.

So back to the story, we decided to take the eight hour trip. She packed goodies and some nice tunes for the ride.

When I went to get her, she only had a book bag packed to go.

I looked around searching for the rest of her bags since we were going on a pretty long road trip.

When I mentioned it to her she laughed it off and said if she needed something she would go home and get it.

I thought she was kidding, so I laughed along with her and made sure I grabbed the snacks.

We were barely out of the state when she started panicking. "Where are you going?" she asked as I looked around wondering if someone else was in the car with us.

"What do you mean? We are going to Pennsylvania" I responded laughing at her performance. "Yeah, but you're about to leave North Carolina!" she said yelling.

I looked at her for at least a minute. "You do realize that Pennsylvania is eight hours away from here right? It's in another state," I said as I watched her expression turn from panic to embarrassment.

"Oh my goodness" she said laughing. I teased her about that for 16 hours, from the time we left until I pulled into her driveway.
I love meeting different people.

As long as you have a discerning spirit you are able to have fun with all types of people.

I had a date with one girl; I used to call her Greedy Gus. I mean she was like a Hoover vacuum cleaner when it came to food.

Fellas, she was the kind of woman that I called "the Matrix."

She was a tiny petite woman. She didn't weigh over 90 pounds and she could literally put a buffet out of business.

I invited her to my house for a little visit. She was a nice girl and I had fun with her, so I overlooked the gluttony.

I asked her if she wanted something to eat and of course she did. I baked her some French fries and chicken nuggets and we ate together.

This was around the holidays, so my mother baked a cake and told us not to touch it. After a brief lunch, we talked for a moment in the kitchen. I stepped away for a few minutes to use the bathroom.

Imagine my surprise when I returned to find her wiping cake crumbs from her mouth.

I stared in horror at the cake, sitting in the dish missing a huge chunk.

Needless to say, she was not invited back to my mother's again.

COMMUNICATION IS KEY

Wherefore, my beloved brethren, let every man be swift to hear, slow to speak, slow to wrath.

James 1:19

Communication

Life and death of a relationship depends upon the attitudes of those within the relationship.

Communication is the key support of a relationship. Healthy communication involves listening.

This is why the Bible tells us in James 1:19 we must be quick to hear and slow to speak. This is how healthy communication fosters a healthy relationship.

If you cannot communicate with each other, your relationship will surely be doomed. We already know that a relationship must be Godly in order to thrive and be successful.

In fact, the foundation of a successful marriage is built upon having knowledge of Christ and a love for Christ.

Every relationship must have a purpose. Relationships in Christ are influential. Your relationship sets an example just as your own behavior does.

Remember, idle relationships breed trouble. Idle relationships are those that do not grow in the knowledge of Christ.

You will find out a lot about a person as they communicate and talk to you.
No one comes with directions.

Wouldn't it be great to meet someone and they reached in their pockets and pulled out directions on how to deal with them?

No one will do that. In fact, when you first start communicating with someone they are going to tell you great things about themselves.

They are going to literally sell themselves to you. They aren't going to tell you about the bad things.

They're not going to say, "Hey, I'm a liar" or "Hi, my name is Marsha and I'm manipulative" It doesn't work that way. It would be great if it did. When you first meet a person it's similar to an interview.

They're going to tell you how their ex hurt them in their last relationship. They will give you the whole sad song.

Listen carefully. A person will give you clues on who they really are by simply talking. Have them talk and listen, you will pull something out.

The best communication comes from God. You have to ask God to show you the person in the beginning.

You need God to be your eyes and ears. First, you need a relationship with God.

As I said before, your relationship with God must be stable if you want a stable relationship with anyone else.

God can't warn you if you can't hear his voice or feel his presence in your heart. Your relationship with God is your prerequisite to your relationship with your mate. This is your protection, because we can't be everywhere.

We can hide in the bushes with camouflage and fatigues on trying to catch someone.
Ladies will get all high tech and unscramble passwords to find out what their man is up to.
Ladies will be checking cell phones, trying to find out who their really dealing with.
If we are dating ladies, you don't have to worry about that with me.

When you are looking for something, you will find something.

The best thing to do is communicate with the lady or gentleman and ask God to be your eyes and your ears.

This is how you create an environment for healthy communication.

Only God can be everywhere. He can go places that you cannot.

When you first start dating someone you are moved by superficial things. You are looking at how someone makes you feel. How attractive they are.

While doing so, you are overlooking their bad qualities. You need to ask God for a discerning spirit.

A spirit of discernment will warn you when something just isn't right. You will simply know. The only thing about a spirit of discernment is, you must be willing to listen to the spirit.

You can't simply ignore the warnings that are showing up about a person.

That is how misunderstandings begin.
A lot of times we don't stand firmly and communicate with someone.

Down south and southern states it's a compliment for a man to ask a woman on a fishing date. Reason being, when the man is fishing with the woman there are no distractions.

It's just you and your mate. No television, no distractions. You get to learn a lot about the person.

I remember the first girl I fell in love with. Her name was Avril Marlow. I remember when she came around I would suddenly feel butterflies. I was so nervous.

You know how on TV when I guy likes a girl he can't talk around her?
I was so nervous around her that I completely avoided her.

I liked her but I couldn't be around her. I was so infatuated with her, I would go home and practice talking to her in the mirror.

I'd be like, "Hi, Avril how are you?" "Can we study Geometry together?" "How were the grape

Now & Later candies that you got from the ice cream truck?"

One day she beat me to the punch. She walked up to me and said, "Hi Sean, how are you?" I instantly started talking like, "I--Hiiiii....tttttt."

After she wiped the spit off her face she walked away. I was so embarrassed. I wanted to transfer to a school two states away. I had trouble communicating with her, because my feelings towards her overwhelmed me.

Then she started dating a friend of mine. Seeing her with this other guy really got to me. It ate me up inside to se her and this guy sharing tater tots and holding hands.

I realized that it was my fault because I never communicated my feelings to her. It finally encouraged me enough to talk to Avril.

Since we both played sports for the Boys and Girls Club her phone number was in the directory. So one day, I mustered enough nerve to call her.

By this time I had an attitude, "Hey, Avril" I said as soon as she answered the phone. "What's up with you going out with my boy Terry Watson?" I told her that I had a crush on her and she said,

"Sean, I didn't know that you felt that way about me." I told her that she broke my heart.

Why did I say that to her?

The next day she told Terry that I said she broke my heart and he told everyone in the school.

The entire school year when my classmates saw me they would sing, "Avril, you broke my heart. Avril, you broke my heart."

So after I got out of counseling.

It took about 17 years of counseling for me to realize that communication is a huge part of a relationship. Whether its to make an existing relationship stronger or to start something new.

I couldn't be angry with Avril for breaking my heart, when really I allowed fear to stop me from asking her out.

I'll give you an example of something that happened to me with regards to non-communication.

My first love and I had trouble with communication.

We ended up on a relationship rollercoaster where we would go together, break up and go together again.

I was becoming very insecure in the relationship because she wouldn't communicate with me. I was sitting in my apartment in the dark, when the Devil came and sat down.

The Devil started communicating with me. He was like, "Hey Sean." I was like "Huh." I answered the Devil because I'm not scared of him.

So he was like, "Remember the answering machine you set up last week?" I said "yeah" he was like, "since you know the code to the answering machine, why don't you listen to them. See what your girl is up to."

I agreed with him and was like, "That's a great idea" so I began to work on the answering machine.

I pulled the answering machine up and the outgoing message began to play, "Hi, this is Kim. I'm not in but please leave me a message"

The first message came on, "Hey, Kim this is Tanya" I skipped over that message. That wasn't the message I was looking for.

The next message began to play, "Hey, Kim this is Sandy.

Girl, I'm trying to see if you want to get your hair done?" I skipped that message. I didn't want to hear that message.

Do you see a pattern here? You know what I was really searching for?

The third message began to play, "Hey Kim, this is Kevin" my heart skipped a beat. "Give me a call at 202…"

I couldn't wait to dial that number back and talk to Kevin.

The phone rang as I started wiping away the sweat. I had finally caught her. "Hello?" someone answered. "Hello? Is this Kevin?" I asked, trying to sound tough.

Now ladies and gentlemen, this is where I need to place my disclaimer.

I was not all the way saved at this point, so what you may read, is not me now.
Don't hold it against me.

"I said stay the ____ away from her because I'm going to put my foot in your _____."

He was like, "Who is this, Sean?" Now at this point my heart is pounding and I'm sweating profusely. How did he already know my name?

I was like "Yeah, who is this?"

"This is Pastor Kevin from over at the church" he said. You know when you get caught in a situation you try to act all spiritual.

I picked myself up off the floor and responded, "Pastor, first giving honor to God our Lord and Savior. I have Tourette's syndrome and I just need you to lift me up in prayer."

The moral to that story is don't go by your own suspicions and make yourself behave crazy.

Communicate with each other.

Dating Their Kids

Remember when you first started dating. It was very simple back then. You exchanged numbers with each other and you talked on the phone for hours.

You wouldn't really talk about anything. The rides that you went to at Kings Dominion the type of movies you loved to see.

Now it isn't so simple.

Once you pass your teens and head into adulthood, you find that many of the people you date will have children from previous relationships.

This isn't a bad thing. In fact, it can be a great thing. Dating a man or woman with children is an interesting thing.

When you begin to date those with ready-made families you not only date the person, you also date their children.

The children are a part of the parent so you know that you will have to date them as well.

I've had friends tell me, "I like the girl, but her kids are Satan." Then you have to make the decision. Do you want Satan in your flock? There is no separation in this. That will filter over in the relationship.

I've seen situations where people will get married and the marriage will be going great, but the children will make the man want to divorce the woman, simply because the woman has no control over her children.

If the relationship continues to grow, but you can't get along with the kids, my advice is to step off.

It won't get any better, because if that parent is a good parent. She is going to send you on your way.

Their kids are a part of them. You can't divorce kids. You will have to impress the kids. Now, I don't mean being a fool, buying toys and clothes and trying to spoil them. Don't try to buy them. The kids are going to look to you to see what they can get out of you. I made that mistake.

I have twin girls. I was dating a nice young lady. She genuinely loved my girls. I could tell that much, but she tried to buy them.

She purchased them like 10 pairs of jeans, five each at their birthday party.

She was my girlfriend and outdid me with the gifts.

She had my family side-eying her because she was new to the family and had purchased more for my children than they had.

I was embarrassed because it didn't seem genuine.

The kids loved her, but it wasn't the real her. She only wanted to buy them.
When we broke up, the kids wanted to call her, especially around Christmas and their birthdays.

I had to stop them and explain to them that they only wanted to talk to her when they could get something from her.

Discussion Questions

How do you feel about dating women/men with children?

What rules do you have about dating someone with children?

Do you have children?

What are your thoughts on your mate meeting your children for the first time?

BE HUMBLE AND GENTLE

"Be completely humble and gentle; be patient, bearing with one another in love. Make every effort to keep the unity of the Spirit through the bond of peace."

Ephesians 4:2-3

The Great Debate

Debating is a huge part of communication in a relationship.

I love to debate with someone because I get the opportunity to hear exactly how they feel. I don't like to be hollered or cursed at but I respect a person's feelings.

Debating gives you an opportunity to know someone's thoughts about a particular subject. When someone opens up to you it gives you a better idea of what they're really going through. We can debate without disrespecting each other. Someone who is quiet, it's cute. A lot of men love quiet women; women who are agreeable.

Men don't want women to nag them and be on their backs, it doesn't help in the relationship. I was in a relationship with a woman who was overly agreeable. If I would say, "Let's jump off the Woodrow Wilson bridge" she would've been all for it. "What time should I be there?"

She agreed with everything that I said. Everything I wanted to do, she was like, "Let's go."

We were in a relationship for nine months. During that entire time I felt like this is the best thing since sweet tea.

She was so agreeable; it was such a pleasant relationship. We had a disagreement and it was over.

I believe the reason was that we didn't have an opportunity to debate anything. We didn't know how to handle an argument.

It's healthy to argue and debate with each other.

I'm not saying every time you see each other you are fighting. Pulling knives on each other and having to call the police.

I'm not suggesting you do that. Arguing is a part of communication. The bible says in, **Ephesians 4:26 – Be ye angry, and sin not: let not the sun go down upon your wrath.**

You must discuss anything that makes you angry with your partner.

Holding on to pain and hurt breeds a root of bitterness in your soul. That is the last thing you need in your life.

If you're in a relationship with someone and you begin to argue, remember that the goal is not to win the argument.

If you find that your goal is to win the argument and not to listen to your significant others' side, you have already lost the argument.

In fact, you are not in alignment with the word of God.

A lot of times we debate because we see things differently. We are different people after all. We are trying to communicate our position.

Real talk, there are times when no matter how hard we try we find ourselves in a place where we are arguing just to win.
We aren't really trying to hear the other side.

We just want to get to a point where we are on common ground with each other.
That's when you have failed at communication.
This is when you need to go into the bible. The bible is your relationship guidebook.

Although the Bible was written thousands of years ago, the premise remains the same. We must love one another.

We must forgive one another. We must treat each other with respect and love.

When love is your common purpose your relationship will be strong enough to withstand debate.

You can discuss things and actually arrive at a conclusion where both sides have a say. Healthy debating in a relationship can be erotic.

It shows the other person that you trust them that you are equally invested and passionate about what they care about.

If you two can work out a conclusion like a team it will take you and you're loved on a journey to a higher level of intimacy.

I love a great debate.

I abhor arguments. I don't like to be in a relationship where the person wants to tell me off.

You know it when the person has an attitude with you when they're speaking with you. Their voice is all high pitched.

They may say something hurtful or say something to upset you. "Your nose is big!"

You knew my nose was big when we first started dating. Why you want to talk about it now?
They will say or do something to make you feel the pain that they are feeling at the moment.
That takes the debate to a different level.

Always debate and argue facts. You can't hurt someone with facts. If you go into the argument to "cut someone up", as we say in DC. You are setting yourself up for failure.

Your debate is unhealthy because of your purpose. You're not a right place.

You want that person to understand where you're coming from. You want them to feel how you felt.

Guess what?

That person wants the same from you they want you to understand where they're coming from. Once the understanding has been reached we can both raise our hands in victory. Remember, a relationship is a team effort. Two are greater than one.

You don't want your team to be weak due to an unresolved issue or an argument gone too far.

THE PURPOSE IN A RELATIONSHIP

Make my joy complete by being of the same mind, maintaining the same love, united in spirit, intent on one purpose.

Philippians 2:2

Purpose in a Relationship

Every relationship must have a purpose. To some people, love is simply a connection; a once in a lifetime moment where time stands still and music begins to play.

Although it sounds lovely, that is simply a fairytale.

Falling in love is like a fairytale but staying in love is nothing like the movies show.

In real life, staying in love takes work, especially if you are an adult with responsibilities and children.

When your relationship has a purpose you have a foundation in which to build your life together.

Some relationships are meant to teach you a lesson in humility, faith, endurance or any trait that God wants to use to refine you.

Other times you enter into relationships that ultimately hurt you.

Those relationships are beneficial to your maturity. You are supposed to learn the lessons that those relationships teach you.

Many see failed relationships as a testament of who they are.

Don't allow those circumstances to enter your heart and make you fear commitment.

I know trusting someone can be scary, but without those lessons you would never be prepared for what's next.

It is because of that failed relationship that you now know what are deal breakers for you. The things that you absolutely won't tolerate are clearer to you.

When God sends your true love, the person that he wants you to create a life with, those lessons will surely come in handy.

Without a purpose in your relationship, you have no common goal. There is nothing in your relationship to hold you there for the long haul.

Some people build their relationships on their children.

Others begin relationships to avoid loneliness. Loneliness can be a huge factor in why some marriages don't last.

Some people, both men and women feel like they should be married and be parents by a certain age.

They have it all mapped out. "By the time I'm 33, I'm going to have 2 kids and be living in this neighborhood with my husband and our German Shepard."

And when 35 rolls around and those things have not happened we panic.

We start to wonder if it will ever happen for us. Especially once we see our friends and family getting married.

It doesn't become serious until your sister or a close relative gets married, then the entire family is looking at you like you're an anemone.

So, you get tired of the questions and finally decide that the next man you date, that isn't a complete serial killer will be the one. Fellas, we are no different. Some of us are also directed by

that big ticking clock in our heads. We wear it
hanging around our necks like Flava Flav.

What do you do when your buddies start to settle
down and you get tired of the single life?
You decide that the next chick you date that
doesn't annoy you will be your wife.
Loneliness is a purpose for a relationship,
although it's not a great purpose.

The purpose of their relationship is to raise and
love their children. But what is your plan when
the children grow up and move on?

What happens to your relationship?

If your partner cheats, has an emotional affair or
does something that you do not agree with, there
is no real commitment no real reason to hold you
two together.

So, ladies and gentlemen, I pose the following
question to you:

What is the purpose of your relationship?
Don't worry if you don't know the answer
immediately.

Many people enter into loving relationships with no real purpose.

They stay together for month's maybe even years, but when things get rough; when trials come their relationship is shaken to the core.

Take some time with your partner and discuss what you think the purpose of your relationship is.

It could be anything.

Find out what they think the purpose of your relationship is to them. This will help you become closer.

Enjoying an adventurous life together is a great example of a purpose. So is having someone to grow spiritually with.

No matter what the purpose of your relationship truly is, I urge you to take some time with your partner and define it.
This will help you grow together. You can see what types of expectations your partner has for your relationship.

If you are dating, does he intend on the relationship leading to marriage.

If you are married what type of purpose can you infuse into your marriage to help strengthen it?

If you are single what purpose would you like to see in your next relationship?

These questions can help you determine if you are ready to take that next step in your relationship.

It will also help you see if you need to move on in your own journey for purpose.

The Unique Relationship

As adults we have all suffered some form of hurt. Whether it was from the hands of someone you knew or some random stranger.

The way in which you deal with those feelings depends upon your childhood. I say that not necessarily to blame your parents or loved ones. In fact no one is really to blame.

Just as we often times become products of our own environment. We also are a reflection of our parent's relationships.

The relationships you watched as a child has a great reflection on how you treat your partner.

If your parents constantly argued and didn't get along very well, you may see that as a normal way to communicate.

In contrast, if your family communicated and talked things out without growing emotional, you may see that as normal.

Normalcy is only relative.
Who really controls the definition of normal?

No matter what you've been through before, you must remember not to bring old hurts into new relationships.

Forgiveness is a gift that you must give to both yourself and the offender. Love is a wonderful thing, but to many it is a risky business deal.
You cannot go into a relationship expecting your partner to be anyone but themselves.

You cannot compare your relationship with anyone else's. Your parents, your friends and those around you all have different relationships.

We must keep in mind that we cannot compare our relationships with anyone else's and we are not defined by anyone's relationship.
Your parents handled situations by screaming, yelling and arguing, does not mean that you will be the same communicator.

You can change the way that you relate to your partner.

The relationship that you are in right now is a unique one. It is unlike any relationship that you have been in before.

Although you have memories of prior relationships, some great some not so great, those memories don't deserve a place in your new relationship.

Remember the lessons, leave the hurt in the past.

You must enter your relationships with a renewed mind and with an expectation of growth.

No two relationships are the same.

Our greatest challenge in a relationship is our view on how it is supposed to appear to others. We look at our friends and loved ones and how their relationships are and determine how ours should be based off their example.

This is a great way to set yourself up for failure. Purpose to find a uniqueness in your relationship and keep it between you and your partner.

There is nothing more seductive in a relationship than a shared secret between you and your loved one, only.

A common thread of purpose and commitment is all you need to see your relationship flourish.

ADAM MADE LOVE TO HIS WIFE,
EVE...

Adam made love to his wife Eve, and she became pregnant and gave birth to Cain. She said, "With the help of the Lord I have brought forth a man."

Genesis 4: 1

Sex & Lust

When we think about making love we don't consider the spiritual aspect of it all. The purpose of making love was to pro-create to share love between each other, but mainly to procreate.

We have changed the meaning and purpose of lovemaking. Lovemaking is now simply an act between two consenting adults. There doesn't have to be any love involved.

Lovemaking has now been replaced by sex. Sex, in my opinion is an act where the essence of love has been removed.

We have all been in situations where we did not make love with someone; we simply had sex with them.

Our hearts weren't in it, we weren't in a relationship with each other or we simply didn't love each other. Lust replaced love.

Lust is a feeling of deep intense desire for something or someone.

Throughout the Bible there are plenty of examples of people allowing their lusts to control their lives.

We all know how some of those experiences ended.

David, the man after God's own heart once allowed lust to control him. Lust had him committing adultery with a married woman.

He even went so far as to having her husband murdered when he learned that Bathsheba was pregnant.

He went to extreme measures to get the woman he wanted and to keep his secret hidden.

Now we are all adults here so I know for sure that many of you have been in situations where lust has driven you to make decisions that you wouldn't ordinarily have made with a sound mind.

I can literally imagine some of you nodding your head as that female or male comes to mind.

Even Solomon wrote about his lust for the woman who stole his affections. In the Song of Solomon, the entire seventh chapter is dedicated to the visual pleasures that this woman gave Solomon.

He spoke of her as if she were a work of art. As if her sexuality was more of a garden of love; something alive and flourishing, yet undefiled.

He wrote, **"Thy navel is like a round goblet, which wanteth not liquor; thy belly is like an heap of wheat set about with lilies. Thy two breasts are like two young roes that are twins"…. Song of Solomon 7:1-9**

If you are ever in need of a love story that will keep your heart pumping, check out the Song of Solomon.

Read it alone, and really allow the words to speak to you. This is truly the most erotic love story in the Bible.

The Bible also tells us that sex before marriage is a sin. I would like to talk about sex with regards to Christian relationships, because we don't want to hear what the word of God says.

1 Corinthians 6:8 – "Every sin that a man doeth is without the body, but he that committeth fornication sins against his own body."

That right there is self-explanatory. There are no loopholes or any way around it. It is what it is.

If you are not married and you are laying down with someone, you know you have no business doing this.

I love to have conversations with others and debate different ideas around.

Recently I met with a group of holy-ghost filled, sanctified ladies and we were discussing relationships.

When our conversation ventured into the arena of sex and the Christian relationship, things got interesting.

They gave me a different perspective on having sex and being saved. They took it back to the beginning, with Adam and Eve.

They said that they never had a wedding. They were not married. God put Adam on the earth and he put Eve on this earth and they co-existed. There was no certificate, no wedding vows. They said that basically, man created the symbol of marriage.

The Bible states that God created man and woman and they simply lived together and loved each other.

They went on to say that if you are committed to someone and you are equally yoked, then you have the green light to have sex.

The argument was interesting; you can claim that man created the pomp and circumstance concerning marriage, but we all know what the Bible says about having sex before marriage.

It makes me pose the question, if you are both Christians walking with God, why don't you want to follow what the Bible says?

It is easy to be committed and then suddenly be un-committed, but when you have taken vows in front of God and witnesses, it is a big deal.

If you are simply dating someone and you want to break up, there is no commitment there.

You start asking for your UNO cards back. The puppy that you gave her that's now a dog, you want it all back. The perfume you gave her years ago, "Yeah, I'm going to need that back."

When you are married you are committed. As humans, we are always looking for the loophole the way to get out.

If you are currently struggling with this, you are not alone. As a single man, it has not always been easy.

I had my first sexual encounter at 13 years of age. It is kind of funny, because nothing actually happened but I'll never forget the experience.

This fast girl from my neighborhood told me that she was going to give me some. I quickly agreed and set up a time for us to make it happen.

She came to my house and we went to the basement. My mother was upstairs. This is my first real encounter with sex. Everything was going great until she began to undress.

The moment she took her pants off an odor filled the room that was reminiscent of the Wharf. Here in the Washington DC area we shop for fresh seafood at the Wharf. You can find all types of crustaceans and fish.
She had my room smelling like the entire fish market. It smelled like raw seafood.

My basement was funktified. The smell was so bad it went through the vents.

My mother came to the landing of the basement and yelled down, "Sean, what did I tell you about eating food in the basement. Bring that food up here!" she demanded.

I didn't know what to do. There wasn't any food, it was the girl. I couldn't tell my mother the real source of the smell, so I did what any rational person would do in that situation.

I searched for a plate and a fork to take back upstairs to play it off. Let's just say, that situation prolonged my chastity for seven years.

I lost my virginity when I was 20. Some may say that, that's a pretty old age to lose your virginity, but you don't know my mother.

When I was a teenager, I wrecked a car in the driveway. My mother was so angry. You know how parents are when you do something bad. She was on the phone telling everyone what I did. She called my grandparents, her friends, our family and some people she didn't even know; she just had to tell someone.

My mother said, "What's next? Are you going to bring a baby home?" I didn't understand how she went from me wrecking a car to bringing a baby home.

So she told me that if I came home with a baby, I would have to find somewhere else to live. That was all I needed to hear. I was shook up.

Suddenly, the idea of sex wasn't as interesting to me.

A WAY OUT OF TEMPTATION

There hath no temptation taken you but such as is common to man: but God is faithful, who will not suffer you to be tempted above that ye are able; but will with the temptation also make a way to escape, that ye may be able to bear it.

1 Corinthians 10:13

Temptation

I'm not a drinker or a smoker. I don't care for alcohol, weed or gambling chips; I'm not interested in those things.

I have three children. One of my children was born in wedlock and the other two were not. Sexual sin is my biggest sin.

An articulate, attractive woman will be on my mind forever. This is my biggest sin. I am susceptible to a lovely face and a brilliant mind.

We all suffer through our flesh. We all want to "get some."

The biggest thing is temptation. It's not sex, itself. It's temptation. Don't set yourself up for the temptation.

If you are with someone and you are very attracted to a person, don't be over their house late.

I'm going to be for real; I like legs and a big behind. If a woman is saved and physically attractive, I'm interested, but I can't put myself in situations where I will fail.

I was in a relationship where I was attracted to a woman. She was beautiful, had a nice home.

We were enjoying ourselves together and she wanted me to spend the night. It would be cool to wake up together and everything, but it wasn't a good thing.

We were setting ourselves up for failure.

I feel like God looks upon us to see if we are trying, but when you walk into a situation that is no good and you know it's no good, you're setting yourself up.

That's like being a recovering crack addict and returning to the crack house to check up on everyone. "Hey, how is everyone? Any new crack out there? How is the crack going?"

You are not in a great situation. You know for sure that you are setting yourself up for a bad situation.

If you are on a diet and trying to lose weight you are not going to hang with your friends at the all you can eat buffet. The temptation is too strong.

I think sexual immorality has a lot to do with temptation.

The times that I have fallen, I never set out searching for the temptation.

I was dating this pretty young lady and we decided to meet for brunch.

We had a great time together so she invited me back to her place to watch some movies.

By the evening we were spooning. Then one thing led to another and I fell.

Most of us, when we are trying to live for God, we don't plan for it, but the temptation comes. We have to guard ourselves.

You have some people living for God who decide that they are going to fall, then claim "God knows my heart"

Yeah God knows your heart, but he also knows that when you get the opportunity you're going to do it again.

I was one of those people. I was all, "Lord, please forgive me" each time I had sex, but then when the temptation came again. I was ready to have sex again.

Ceiling fans and sex go hand and hand for me, because after sex, I would stare at that fan.
As I stared at the fan, watching it twirl around, I found myself repeating, "I'm sorry God." You can always ask God for forgiveness. God is a forgiving God, but he wants to be able to trust us.

Just like a human. If one of my friends stole from me, and I let it go and he does it again and again. How trusting will I be of that person?

God knows our heart and every hair on our head. He knows that we will set out and do it again after asking for forgiveness.

What are your thoughts?

How do you feel about temptation?

What is a temptation that you are most susceptible to?

BELIEVE NOT EVERY SPIRIT

Beloved, believe not every spirit, but try the spirits whether they are of God: because many false prophets are gone out into the world.

1 John 4:1

Spirits and Sex

Some theologians believe that when you have sex with someone, their spirits attaches to you.

If you can take a moment and think about the people that you have had sex with, all of those spirits lie within you.

So in their theory, if you are struggling with issues or going crazy, just imagine you could be dealing with a spirit from someone that you had sex with.

You could have had a one-night stand with people you don't know and their spirits have attached to you.

If you have had sex with 50 different people, you could possibly have 50 different spirits attached to your own.

I would love to hear your thoughts on this topic. *This is also a great discussion topic for a couple or group.*

Discussion Questions

How do you feel about this theory?

What are your thoughts on spirits attaching themselves to you through sex?

Could this be why we are not to fornicate?

Masturbation

Now I know what you are thinking, "Come on Sean, really?" but this topic needs to be discussed.

If we are being honest with each other on this quest for the Godly relationship, we have to touch subjects that seem taboo.

A lot of times we say, "well, if I'm not having sex with anyone or bringing anyone into my sin, masturbation should be fine", but God wants our minds to be pure.

Sex is all around us. If you are watching shows like Empire on regular television you are watching sex.

If you find yourself up late at night watching the movie channels, guess what? It's porno time. SpongeBob the movie now becomes, "its porno time!"

Sex is thrown in our face all day everyday. Why? Because we all know that sex sells. Sexual immorality is all around us. The Internet makes it even harder for you. We must guard ourselves from sexual images.

When we are trying to live for God and do the right thing that is when the moment of temptation happens.

You are watching television, the mood is right and BAM it hits you. You feel your nature rising and you decide to get to know yourself a little better. God wants to know if your mind is pure. He wants to know if your heart is pure.

Some may say, "Well I'm not hurting anyone." But what is your reason for masturbation? Sometimes it's boredom. You have nothing else to do so you decide to please yourself. An idle mind is the devil's workshop. When our minds are idle we do things that we shouldn't.

Sometimes we need to release tension. Some say, they're getting the edge off. You can get the edge off yourself, but remember God is a jealous God.

He wants you to talk to him. Go to him with your problems.

Philippians 4:6, tells us to pray about everything and worry about nothing.

If you have tension in your life, bills high, money low, kids running amuck that does not give you the green light to masturbate and get the tension off.

I was using masturbation to fall asleep. Forget about a hot toddy or Nyquil. I didn't need the nighttime, coughing, and sore throat medicine to rest.

When I couldn't sleep, I just went to get to know myself a little better.

God wants you to turn all things over to him. I know that I have put a pin in your balloon, but it's not right.

When we are masturbating we are not thinking about what we should have our minds on. We are not thinking about the taxes when we masturbate.

We are not thinking about the kids, well I hope not!

We are not thinking about anything of substance. In fact, we are usually thinking of something erotic when we masturbate.

We are thinking about someone that we are not married to; we are not thinking about anything good.

94

We need to keep our thoughts on God and on pleasing him.

These are things we must consider.

Discussion Questions

What are your thoughts on masturbation?

Do you consider masturbation a sin?

JEALOUSY IS CRUEL AS THE GRAVE

Set me as a seal upon thine heart, as a seal upon thine arm: for love is strong as death; jealousy is cruel as the grave: the coals thereof are coals of fire, which hath a most vehement flame.

Song of Solomon 8:6

Jealousy

There is no room for jealousy in a relationship.

As I've demonstrated in my prior stories, jealousy will have you doing things you never thought of.

I still can't believe that I cursed at Pastor Kevin like that.

Jealousy in a relationship stems from a lack of trust.

If you have trust issues in your relationship, they must be dealt with in order to continue in a healthy relationship.

Once the trust has been damaged, there is no going back.

You must try to repair the trust by revving up the communication with each other.

You need to discuss what occurred in the relationship to cause the breakdown of trust. You must dig deep and make the investment in your relationship, especially if you really love this person.

Anger, resentment and distrust will build a root of bitterness in your spirit.

That is the last thing you want to deal with.

Not only will your relationship suffer, but you will find yourself at the defensive end of every conversation.

Every single time your hands touch the doorknob; your mate will be standing at the door with questions.

"Where are you going?"
"With who?"
"When are you coming back?"

And no matter how respectfully and truthfully you answer the question, her response will be, "Hmm…."

There is literally no escaping it.

Ladies, you are not immune to this. If there is a trust issue in your relationship you are charged with working it out.

Your man will be asking you those questions and still have on a face mask and a helmet hiding in the bushes with binoculars.

You don't want your man tracking you down, hiding in the bushes in camouflage. You want him to believe that when you say something, you are telling him the truth. Many relationships have imploded due to the lack of trust.

Social Media

Our generation has been blessed and cursed through the invention of technology. Computers and the Internet have increased the efficiency in the way we all live and work.

Many of us couldn't complete our jobs without a computer and Internet access.

In 2004, when Facebook was first launched no one would have imagined that it would be where it is today.

We wouldn't have even considered going online to change our relationship status when we make it official with that special someone.

We wouldn't have imagined going online to meet someone new to love, but here we are. We spend our lives and relationships tethered to the Internet.

Social media applications such as Facebook, Instagram and Twitter were all created for us to stay in touch. We can reach people clear across the world if we need to.

Social networks have even changed the way we communicate with our families and friends. Instead of grabbing the phone to wish someone a happy birthday, we now post it on Facebook.

Websites like Black Planet, eHarmony and Black People Meet have taken the place of the local bar or club.

Social media has become the preferred method of dating these days.

People get to know each other online months before they meet in person. Some people go years.

Some of us go online searching for the special person and find that the person on the other end of the computer is a poser.

In fact, a lot of people are on social media sites posing. They have scriptures on their page, polished pretty headshots and everything they can to make themselves look great.

You can learn a lot about someone online based on the things they post and their behavior. They will post their jobs and the things they do as recreation.

If you are dating someone and you both are on social media here a few red flags to watch out for:

102

- Their relationship status remains the same, "Single"
- Their page is filled with selfies and no pictures of you or the two of you together
- They are only liking pictures of people from the opposite sex
- Now I understand if you are an entertainer or a business owner. Your Facebook friend situation may be a little different, like mine. But if you are working at the Post office and you have 2,000 friends and 1,999 of them are women, there may be a problem.

I use social media to post pictures of me with my fans and share information about tour dates.

While I don't mind being in a relationship and posting on social media sites, there are a few things that unnerve me.

The person who likes to post updates of our relationship, every minute of our relationship.

I don't want the world to know that I bought you flowers on your birthday or that I forgot your birthday entirely.
Social media is not the place to air your dirty laundry.

I have friends right now, which I communicate better via text or Facebook than over the phone. I can admit that I communicate with fans, friends and family over social media more than anywhere.

It is a highly useful tool, but it does make me wonder a few things about the affects of social media on relationships.

Remember life before social media? Do you remember how we communicated with the opposite sex?

Passing notes in school and talking all night on the phone with the music playing in the background; those were the days.

I have a story about dating before social media. My cousin and I were talking to these girls over the phone. I don't know how we exchanged numbers but we ended up talking for a while.

We were about 13 years old. We thought they were cute and they thought we were cute so we started talking to them.

We decided that we were going to meet them. We lived in Oxon Hill, MD and they lived in South East, DC so we took the bus out to see them.

There was a man on the bus smelling like "boo boo." Me being the comedian, I joked about him. I had everyone on the bus laughing. We had a good time.

We hung with them for a while, talking and chilling outside. All of a sudden, my stomach started rumbling. I looked around and assumed that I had to pass gas.

Then my stomach made another move and I realized I needed to use the bathroom. I realized that this was a serious situation.

I went to the girl and asked her if I could use her bathroom. She told me that she wasn't going all the way upstairs so I could go to the bathroom.

I told her that I didn't have to go do a number one I needed to do a number six. It was serious. She handed me a ring of keys like she was a janitor. She had 80 keys on the key ring. I walked to the 13th floor and searched through the keys looking for the one to open her door.

I finally open the door to the right apartment and start scrambling, searching for the bathroom. I go in the bathroom and tried to take off my pants in the front of the toilet and by then it was on its way.

I tried to swing around to sit on the toilet because I was facing it.

Why did I miss the toilet?

I had messed all around the side of the toilet. I'm sitting here in disgust, like I can't believe I messed this bathroom up like that.

Me, being the brilliant 13 year old that I was, I took a big wad of toilet paper like a baseball to clean the mess, then I flushed it.

When I flushed the toilet the paper wouldn't go down. The water started overflowing in the toilet.

I started panicking looking for something to use. I noticed a fish net sitting in a bucket and used that to remove the debris. Panicking, I threw the debris out the window.

At this point, I can hear kids screaming, "eww somebody is throwing doo doo out here."

I was so miserable at this point. I wanted to just hide. Then I heard a knock at the bathroom door. It was the girl's mother.

I looked at my watch and realized that I had been in the bathroom for over 45 minutes.

She knocked, "Baby, you've been in there a while. I have to use the bathroom honey" I panicked even more and started using anything I could find to get the doo doo and debris up.

I used their pantyhose, towels, washcloths,
anything that I could find.
It was on the ceiling and the walls.

When the mother jimmied the door with a credit
card, and threw open the door, she started
screaming.

"Get out of my house!" I didn't know what to do.
My cousin was in the hall talking to the other girl.
I yelled to him that we had to go. He started
running behind me.

As we ran to the bus stop he smelled me and was
like, "did you boo boo on yourself?"
I didn't even answer him.

Needless to say, I am grateful that these days we
can meet people online in the privacy of our own
bathrooms.

Discussion Questions

Does social media play a role in failed relationships?

Does Facebook affect the way we show love to our partners?

BAGGAGE IS BONDAGE

Stand fast therefore in the liberty wherewith Christ hath made us free, and be not entangled again with the yoke of bondage.

Galatians 5:1

Baggage & Forgiveness

Often times in relationships we find ourselves holding onto unsolved business from the previous relationship. We enter into re-bound love and immediately jump into a relationship.

As a Christian we are called to forgive. No matter what someone has done to you, no matter the circumstance we are to forgive others as Christ forgave us.

I know sometimes forgiveness can be a bitter pill to swallow, but it must be done. There are people reading this book who have experienced hard times at the hand of others.

Women who have been subjected to all sorts of emotional, physical and sexual abuse. I am in no means trying to minimize the trauma that you experienced, but I must tell you to forgive.

Males have also been betrayed? We have experienced situations where women have lied to us. You say that's it. I'm done with this person and you move on.

A lot of times we have not really forgiven that person. We enter in the new relationship with baggage.

I've had a lady tell me that I reminded her of her ex-husband because of where I stood or sat in her house. If I walked around her house and went into a room, she would have a problem. She had too much baggage.

All of us have baggage. Even if you have children, they are baggage.

When you enter into a relationship, you have children and the other person may not. You want the person to like the children and the children to like them, but that can be baggage.

It's hard for me to say, especially since I have three girls. I have baggage. But my baggage MUST be accepted.

Before you move into a new situation, please make sure that the previous situation has been solved.

We are always the victims. When we tell the story, we talk about the bad things they did. We never stop and look at ourselves and admit our wrongs.

We never say, "I was the negative piece in the relationship."

If you continue to talk about what the other person did wrong, the person you speak to may soon wonder what you did to cause this.

No one comes out of a bad relationship smelling like a rose. Everyone has done something to a degree.

It could have been impatience with the person who had the issue. Where you didn't have the patience to pray to God and ask God to allow you to be their backbone.

A lot of times when things don't work out we run.

The next relationship that we run to we end up taking the baggage to that one. By the time we look up, our backs are broken from the baggage that we carry.

If you want good things in your life, you must invite them in. You must also invite the bad things to leave.

Ask God to cleanse you of you hurts and pains. When we pray and ask God to work on us and to create a clean heart in us, he answers us. We feel a sense of peace where there was once pain.

We see the past for what it was, a learning experience and we grow beyond it.

Make it your purpose in life to let go of what weighs you down. God intends for us to have an abundant life. When he speaks of abundance, he is not speaking of materialistic things.

God wants us to have a life filled with abundant joy, abundant peace, and abundant love. Don't allow hurt, baggage and bitterness to block those abundant blessings.

Drop the bags.

HIS PLANS ARE BETTER THAN YOURS

For I know the thoughts that I think toward you, saith the Lord, thoughts of peace, and not of evil, to give you an expected end.

Jeremiah 29:11

It's My Time

The older we grow the more dedicated we become to our internal clock. I'm not referring to the clock that has you waking up at 6am on your day off.

I'm referring to the internal clock attached to the checklist that we all create for ourselves.

Sometimes others have created our checklists for us. This checklist includes marriage, children, a great career and home ownership.

Some people drive themselves crazy trying to obtain everything on their checklist, at the expense of their own happiness.

I'm sure many of you know what I'm talking about. When your twenties are a distant memory and you find yourself staring down your mid thirties.

The checklist is highlighted and imprinted in your brain.

The biggest strain on your mentality is when the wedding and baby shower invitations start pouring in.

You find yourself staring at your 35-year-old reflection in the mirror questioning your happily ever after.

Your best friend is married with children, your cousins are having children, and even your high school buddies are married.

You start to wonder, "When is it my time?" We must understand that it's not in our time; it's in God's own time.

When you try to jump ahead of God's timing you put yourself at risk of heartbreak.

Many of us are in bad relationships right now because we felt that it was our time and we jumped ahead of God's timing.

Your life is shaped by your decisions. When you prophesize over your own life and decide that it's your time, you make rash decisions.

I understand that you want to be a parent. You want to give your parents grandchildren, but you must wait for God.

I was one of those people who declared that it was my time. I was ready for a family.

I found myself having sex with someone that I didn't really know.

I met this young lady in the middle of October, by the second week in December she was pregnant.

A lot of people fall into what I consider, situationships. That's exactly what I fell into.

When you meet someone and before you really know each other, you have a baby. That's a situation-ship.

Now I told myself that it was my time. I believed it.

Although I love my children, I wish that I had them under better circumstances.
I wish they were born out of a loving marriage and not a situation-ship.

A lot of us get married and we feel as though it's our time, but what does God say? It may be your time, but it might not be your time with that person.

My favorite scripture is, **Matthew 6:33 –** "Seek ye first the kingdom of God." God knows your heart. He knows what you need.

That's why it's best to wait on God. You may feel like it's your time, but wait on the Lord.

Jumping into marriages will have you miserable and attached to someone who is no good for you. You could jump into a situation with someone who is simply looking out for themselves. Only God knows.

About the Author

For over 20 years Sean Sarvis has been perfecting his walk with God while simultaneously tickling the funny bones of saints across the world.

He has a passion that is unique to the entertainment industry, in that he doesn't need profane rhetoric or vulgarity to keep you laughing out loud!

Sean has mastered the craft of taking you on a humorous journey...at the same time providing you with gut-busting laughter, and assisting you to visualize a story or scenario as if you were at the scene.

As a writer, producer and director of his own material, he has become a triple threat in the industry. Sean's walk to comedy greatness began in the suburbs of Washington, DC, in a place called Temple Hills, Maryland.

While attending Crossland High School, Sean was universally known as the student who could not keep quiet during class. So, in a brazen attempt by his art teacher to buy his silence, he was offered a "5 minute" deal to perform at the end of the class.

That was Sean's first deal and the deal that he most appreciates because he realized at that moment that making people laugh was his gift.

Sean went on to attend Bowie State University after high school. On a dare from a classmate, during his freshmen year, he performed at a talent show for homecoming.

His performance went off without a hitch, which further affirmed his belief that this was his calling.

Sean's journey began as a secular comedian in the early '90's in the Washington, DC area.

He appeared six times on BET's Comic View and toured with fellow comedian, actress and Oscar Award Winner Monique for two years. He has opened for the comedians who toured on the infamous Kings of Comedy tour, namely Steve Harvey, DL Hughley, Cedric the Entertainer and the late great Bernie Mac.

Venues for his numerous appearances include BET's Teen Summit, Gospo Centric's "Soulaughable", Charles Kane's "God Ain't No Joke" and numerous colleges, universities, and military bases worldwide.

He was named 'Comedian of the Year' in 1996 in the Washington, DC Metropolitan area Glynn Jackson Productions.

While on tour the majority of his audiences didn't know that Sean was a born-again Christian. He received Christ at the tender age of 14.

As he gained notoriety, he was also feeling conflicted in his spirit about having profanity in his material.

After an appearance at the world-famous Lincoln Theatre in Washington, DC in 2001, a six year old approached Sean after a show and repeated his entire routine from a previous performance on Comic View…profanity and all.

Sean recalls that "aha moment", "It was in that moment that I felt something had to change in me. If I am to be an ambassador for Christ I have to walk the walk and most importantly talk the talk." Shortly following that revelation, Sean set his sights on becoming a world-famous Christian comedian.

Stepping out on faith, he produced his first Christian Comedy show at Glendale Baptist Church (The Sanctuary) in Glenarden, Maryland. Sean's journey continues!

For three years, Sean was a staple on an established gospel radio station in Washington, DC, Heaven 1580AM, where he wrote and produced "The Sarvis Report" for the morning show.

His unique knack for creating characters was showcased with characters like, Lewis the Cat and Miss Irene.

Sean has had the pleasure of working with a host of industry greats in the secular and gospel community like, Kevin Hart, Mike Epps, Byron Cage, Tye Tribbett, Ricky Dillard, Kanye West, Rickey Smiley, J.B. Smooth, Cheryl "Salt" James, Stacy Lattisaw, Yolanda Adams, Mary Mary, Kirk Franklin, Canton Jones, Ki Ki Sheard, Dorinda Clark-Cole, Regina Belle, J.J. Harriston, Jonathan Slocumb, Marcus D. Wiley, James Fortune, Ernest Pugh, Martha Muninzi, Kurt Carr, Tanya DallasLewis, Vickie Winans, Marvin Sapp, Smokie Norful....just to name a few.

Sean has been featured on Gospo Centric's Inspirational Comedy DVD, as well as Sony Music's DVD entitled "Soulaughable." In 2010, Sean became a regular entertainer on Radio One's "Family Comedy Tour."

The success of Sean's performances on the DVD's and tours widened his fan base and garnered a huge following.

Sean hit another career milestone in 2010 when he became the executive producer of "DA Block Party", a television show which featured the who's who of Christian Comics in this country. Some of the featured artists included, Marcus D. Wiley, Small Fire, Chinnitta Morris aka "Chocolate", Joe Recca, Mike Washington and Rod Z. Also highlighted on "DA Block Party" were musical guests Blount 2 Blount

(Tanya Blount and Willie Blount) and Christian rapper King Solomon.

Since 2010, Sean has been performing at local and national events. Sean produces comedy shows in the Washington, DC metropolitan area to sell-out crowds. Sean has been a frequent guest on both the WTTG Fox 5 and WUSA Channel 9 morning shows.

For those who do not know Sean Sarvis, he is a man of God first. Secondly he is the father of twin girls Sydney and Shawna and his baby daughter Riann. Thirdly, he is the son of Linda Walker and Jerry Sarvis.

For others who wish to know his talent, understand that you cannot discuss Christian Comedy in the Washington, DC metropolitan area without mentioning Sean Sarvis.

Over the past decade, Sean has been a pioneer Christian Comedian who spreads laugher locally and nationally to people of all walks of life.

His comedic genius is straight from God who grants him the use of clean, animated and downright hilarious material! And for that he is THANKFUL!

The next level for Sean is to produce and direct Christian television shows, Christian music videos and movies for generations to enjoy. Some of Sean's material can be found on YouTube. Sean is a comedian for life who believes the purpose of his gift is to add joy to the lives of those who need, want and desire it.

He leans on the scripture Proverbs 17:22 "A merry heart doeth good like medicine...." "I thank God for providing me the medicine to minister to His people" he says.

www.ingramcontent.com/pod-product-compliance
Lightning Source LLC
Chambersburg PA
CBHW052033270326
41931CB00012B/2474